Text copyright © 2021 by Claire Saxby
Illustrations copyright © 2021 by Cindy Lane

First US edition 2023
First published by Walker Books Australia 2021

Library of Congress Catalog Card Number 2022936747
ISBN 978-1-5362-2503-7

23 24 25 26 27 28 LEO 10 9 8 7 6 5 4 3 2 1

Printed in Heshan, Guangdong, China

This book was typeset in Alegreya and Gararond.
The illustrations were created with seawater, found natural pigments,
watercolors, pencil, pastel, digital drawing, and digital collage.

Candlewick Press
99 Dover Street
Somerville, Massachusetts 02144

www.candlewick.com

GREAT WHITE
SHARK

CLAIRE SAXBY
ILLUSTRATED BY CINDY LANE

CANDLEWICK PRESS

From above, her charcoal skin blends in
with the dark depths of the ocean.

Female great white sharks grow about as long as a giraffe is tall and may weigh more than a large car. They have a strong, lightweight skeleton and tiny toothlike scales.

From below,
her white belly
floats pale
against the sky.

8

Great white sharks are mostly loners
and roam widely across oceans.

The great white shark swims on.
Her tail sways side to side;
her fins keep her balanced.
She travels the fast lane
where she can, cruising
invisible seaways.

What is she looking for?

She's looking for food.

She is a silent and powerful submarine
and follows her own maps.

Great white sharks have a sixth sense called
electroreception. This allows them to
detect prey and to navigate.

11

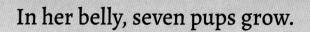

In her belly, seven pups grow.

Female great white sharks
will have between two and
ten pups in a litter.

She circles an island where this year's fur seal pups are learning to swim. There are other sharks here, but she mostly ignores them. The water is cool, and her body temperature adjusts so she stays warm.

Warmer muscles mean more power and more speed. This is particularly important when hunting.

She quiets, all senses alert.
There . . . a dawdling pup. She surges. Fast.
Too fast for the pup to see her until it is too late.

Like cheetahs, great white sharks are
fast and powerful hunters.

As the fur seals grow faster and
smarter, the great white shark
travels north. She swims steadily
hour after hour. It's a long journey,
but she remembers the way.

She's trekking to warmer waters
that teem with fish.
Her pups will thrive there.

Great white sharks have two types of
muscles—one type for slow swimming,
the other for short, powerful strikes
on prey. They can travel up to
50 miles (80 kilometers) per day.

A shadow passes overhead.
It could be a carcass, a meal
she doesn't need to hunt.
She bites, spits it out.

Great white sharks' taste buds are thought
to identify only "food" or "not food."
Sharks have many rows of sharp,
serrated teeth but cannot chew.

She alters her path, follows a scent only she can smell, movements only she can feel.

Great white sharks can smell live prey from far away.

She gathers, explodes
upward, seizes a turtle.
She bites. Swallows.
Her bite is stronger
than that of a lion.

She digests her meal as she journeys on.
When she is done, she vomits what she can't use.

Great white sharks can turn their stomach almost inside out to expel bones and shell fragments.

Unseen, somewhere far from shore, she births her pups.

Very little is known about where great white sharks give birth. Pups at birth may be up to 5 feet (1.5 meters) in length and must immediately look after themselves.

If you find her pups, you will not find her.
She is gone.

Is she looking for you?
No. Never.

27

INFORMATION ABOUT GREAT WHITE SHARKS

Sharks are one of the oldest creatures on our planet. They have roamed our oceans for millions of years. Great white sharks are among the largest ocean predators (second only to killer whales), though there are larger sharks. They have no permanent home and traverse temperate and tropical waters but may return annually to favorite hunting grounds. They grow slowly and have relatively long life-spans—forty years or more for females and seventy years or more for males. Young great white sharks have narrow teeth and feed on fish and rays. When they are about 10 feet (3 meters) in length, their teeth become wider, with serrated edges. Their diet also alters to include dolphins, sea lions, and turtles.

Despite widespread fear, humans are more likely to be struck by lightning than attacked by a great white shark. Sharks have much more to fear from humans: ocean pollution, illegal hunting, commercial fishing, and shark nets.

INDEX

Look up the pages to find out about all these great white shark things.
Don't forget to look at both kinds of words—this kind and this kind.